Teaching with Robert Munsch Books

Amy von Heyking
and
Janet McConaghy

SCHOLASTIC
PROFESSIONAL BOOKS

Scholastic Canada Ltd.

Toronto New York London Auckland Sydney
Mexico City New Delhi Hong Kong Buenos Aires

Table of Contents

The Story of Robert Munsch

Robert Munsch was born on June 11, 1945, in Pittsburgh, Pennsylvania. Surrounded by eight brothers and sisters, he claims that he had to develop a strange sense of humour to get some attention. Though he had difficulty at school, he read a lot and wrote many poems. While studying to become a Jesuit priest, he earned a History degree and an M.A. in Anthropology. During this period, he worked part-time at an orphanage. When he decided to leave the Jesuits, he took a job at a daycare to make some decisions about his future. He decided that his future was in daycare.

When he started telling stories to children, he found out that he was very good at it. He made up many stories, but never wrote them down. Then he and his wife moved to Canada and worked at the preschool at the University of Guelph in Guelph, Ontario. With the encouragement of a children's librarian, Robert finally wrote several of his stories down and sent them to publishers. One was accepted for publication by Annick Press — *The Mud Puddle.* He published more stories, and eventually gave up his daycare job in order to write and tell stories full-time.

Sometimes, ideas come from Robert's family and home life; he has written stories about his three children — Julie, Andrew, and Tyya. And writing full-time has given him the freedom to travel, meet interesting people, and find inspiration for more stories. Typically, Robert Munsch will visit a school or class that has written him an interesting letter. (He does not schedule these visits ahead of time and usually arrives unannounced.) There he will spontaneously make up a story about someone in the audience who has caught his eye. Sometimes these original stories are very good; sometimes they're not. The good ones he'll remember. He always asks for a photograph of the child who inspired the story so he can keep the photograph and the story idea in his files. He will often tell a story many times before he is satisfied that it is ready to become a book. Then he will share the photograph and inspiration behind the story with the illustrator, so that he or she can use that information for reference.

Robert Munsch has visited many places in Canada and the United States, and has even stayed with the people who became characters in his books. There really is a Moira in Hay River, NWT, who was the inspiration for *Moira's Birthday*, and a visit with Julia Muckpah in Arviat, Nunavut, provided the background for *A Promise Is a Promise*. In this guide you'll discover the story behind each of the six books featured.

Munsch has written more than forty books which have sold tens of millions of copies, making him Canada's best-selling author. He has met many more children who have inspired stories, but their books have not yet appeared. With so many stories yet to be told, children can be confident that there are many more laughs to come with Robert Munsch.

MUNSCH MERITS

Some parents may express concern about the "tone" of Munsch books. Emphasize that:

- ❷ the humour comes from exaggeration, which has great appeal for children.

- ❷ the stories take a zany approach to familiar childhood experiences; they are fantasy, and children understand this.

- ❷ the humour often depends on situations where children get the better of their parents or other authority figures. This kind of role reversal is fun for children.

- ❷ children learn how the language and the illustrations combine to capture the playfulness of the stories.

Robert Munsch Q & A

Q: "Why did you want to become a writer?"
Myles, Grade 3

A: "I became a writer so kids could hear my stories even if I was not telling them. I also hoped it would be fun, and it is."

Q: "Where do you get your ideas for your books?"
Crystal

A: "Ideas sort of just happen to me. The last story I made up was about a kid named A.J. He was in the story because he stuck up his hand when I said, "Who wants to be in a new story?" I already knew what the story was about when I asked who wanted to be in it, because I was in a school library that was full of CHOCOLATE BARS because the school was selling chocolate bars. So I knew I was going to do a chocolate bar story, but I didn't know what the story would be. It turned out to be a neat story. I was in that school library because I was driving by and did a quick visit because the school had written me five years in a row. I was not PLANNING to do a new story. It just happened. I just mailed A.J. the story and asked him for his picture in case the story ever becomes a book."

Q: "Are the people you write about in your family?"
Taz, Grade 3

A: "Some of the people I write about are in my family. Julie in *David's Father*. Tyya in *Something Good*. Andrew in *Andrew's Loose Tooth*. The kids in the other books are usually the kid I first made the story up for."

Q: "How do you get inspired to be so creative? I really like your writing."
Hailey, Grade 2

A: "To get inspired I tell stories in schools or daycares and visit families. Doing things like that gets me inspired. Only I can't trust inspiration. When I get inspired I make up stories. Unfortunately, a lot of them are no good. When I tell stories to kids, the kids nicely show me which ones are not good by making noise or otherwise misbehaving. For a good story kids will be quiet, or only make noise when the story wants them to."

Q: "We have been studying your books all week, which is a long time, when you're in kindergarten. We would like to know how long it takes you to write a book, from start to finish."
St. Margaret's School, Kindergarten

A. "It takes me at least two years to finish a story. *The Paper Bag Princess* took eight years and *Mortimer* took ten years."

Q: "Are any of your stories true?"
Dylan, Grade 2

A: "No. The kids in my books are real even though the stories are not real."

Q: "What do you think makes your books so popular with kids?"
Taylor, Grade 2

A: "I think my books are popular because

they are funny and are about things that kids really care about, like snowsuits and snot and teachers and underwear and junk food and hugs."

Q: "How do you make your books so funny?"
Tyler, Grade 3

A: "I get my stories funny by telling them to kids until they get funny. If they don't get funny, I stop telling them. Making funny stories is strange, because they seem so brainless and funny and simple, but they take me a long time to make. My stories do not start out really funny. They only get really funny after I drag them through a lot of audiences of kids. I am not sure why this works for me and the stories, but it does."

Q: "Why do you write funny books?"
Marie

A: "This is a very good question, because I don't mean to write funny books. It just happens that when I tell stories, the stories are always funny. Even when I try to make them not funny they end up being funny. So — why does my brain work like that? I don't know. Maybe I just like to hear people laugh."

Q: "Why do you usually have Michael Martchenko do your illustrations?"
Kendall, Grade 2

A: "I try to pick the illustrator that best suits the story. Michael's illustrations really suit my stories."

Q: "What is your favourite colour and animal? What book do you think is the scariest and which do you think is the funniest? Which character is your favourite?"
Dakoda, Grade 3

A: "My favourite colour is black, because nobody else has the favourite colour black. My favourite animal is an orange beetle. *A Promise Is a Promise* is my most scary book. *I Have to Go!* is my funniest book. My favourite character is . . . ahh . . . ummm . . . I don't think I have a favourite character."

A Picture of Michael Martchenko

Michael Martchenko has illustrated twenty-nine of Robert Munsch's stories. Their collaboration began when Michael was working at an art studio. The studio put on a show featuring samples of their work and Michael added one of his illustrations to fill in an empty space in the display. It was that illustration — a whimsical picture of birds with landing gear — that caught the eye of Robert Munsch and the editors of *The Paper Bag Princess*. They asked Michael to illustrate that story and a very productive relationship was born!

For several years, Michael worked at an advertising agency during the day and illustrated books evenings and weekends. In 1993 he began to illustrate full-time. He works in a studio at his home. He has illustrated stories by authors such as Allen Morgan, Ardyth Brott and Maxine Trottier as well as the majority of Robert Munsch's books. Students might be interested in seeing a very different side of Michael Martchenko in the illustrations for Linda Granfield's book *High Flight*, the story of World War II RCAF pilot John Magee. This book gave him the opportunity to do the realistic aviation art he loves.

When Michael receives the text of a new Robert Munsch story, he reads it two or three times and quickly begins to sketch the images that come to mind. He makes use of the photographs of the real people and places that inspired the story, and then he lets his imagination run wild. Often ideas for playful details will come to him as he draws. For example, the side story of the fox, rooster and hens in *Playhouse* developed when he happened to draw a hen in an early draft of the illustration. Once he started the story, he had to carry it through the rest of the book to find out what would happen!

Michael enjoys the freedom that Munsch stories offer him. The simplicity of the stories gives him the opportunity to add visual details that he thinks will appeal to children without distracting them from the story itself. Robert Munsch will sometimes even change his stories a bit after he sees the sketches so that the illustrations work better.

The humour of Munsch's stories appeals to Martchenko. When his daughter was young, he used to show her the illustrations to see if she thought they were funny. Now he relies on his own judgment. Based on the reaction of young fans everywhere, he is perfectly attuned to children's sense of humour!

The pterodactyl that has become a hallmark in Munsch books first appeared in *Mmm, Cookies!* At Robert Munsch's suggestion, Martchenko has continued to put one in each book since. Other features in his illustrations that readers should watch for include the covers of other Munsch books, and items that are out of place. What's that chainsaw doing in the kitchen in *Makeup Mess?*

... that Michael Martchenko has also *written* books? He says that he finds it harder to write stories than to illustrate them. But if he writes about something that's tough to draw, he can only blame himself!

"How long does it take you to illustrate a Robert Munsch story?"
"About two months from start to finish."

"Why don't you illustrate all of Robert Munsch's stories?"
"Sometimes there is a story that would better suit someone else's style. Other times I'm too busy. Don't worry, there are more Munsch/Martchenko books coming!"

A Picture of Alan and Lea Daniel

Alan grew up in Belleville and Hamilton, Ontario. He always had a love of books. Often he and his friends would act out their favourite stories. With the encouragement of some experienced illustrators, he took a job making diagrams and maps and learned how to draw and paint. He has illustrated the books of Phyllis Reynolds Naylor, Janet Lunn's *The Story of Canada,* and James Howe's Bunnicula series.

Alan and his wife Lea often share the work of illustrating books. They brainstorm together but divide responsibilities different ways depending on the job. Often, Alan sketches the initial ideas and does the drawings, and Lea does the painting. Alan and Lea have also written and illustrated their own books.

The Daniels have illustrated three Robert Munsch books together — *Good Families Don't, Get Out of Bed!,* and *Aaron's Hair.* Their bright and animated pictures are a wonderful complement to Munsch's wild stories. They say that the best part of illustrating Munsch's books is the fun they have doing it. The hardest part is keeping their silliness in check. They begin with the photographs Robert Munsch provides of the children who inspired the story. They then visualize the story and draw the action from many different angles until they are satisfied they have found the best ones. Often, it helps to hear Robert Munsch tell the story several times, because each time they will hear and picture something different. They include drawings of their own furniture, pets, children, and friends in the details. Sometimes the visual ideas that they have lead to changes or additions in the text.

Take a look

🌀 Alan and Lea Daniel often include their own pets in their illustrations. Look at the illustrations in *Get Out of Bed!* How many pets do you think they have? What kind of pets do they have?

🌀 Visual jokes to watch for include the book the children are reading on page 18, and the picture on the milk carton on page 24. Who do you think that is?

A Picture of Eugenie Fernandes

Eugenie Fernandes grew up in an artistic family. Her father was a comic book artist in the 1930s, and as a child she spent many hours in his studio, drawing. She attended the School of Visual Arts in New York City, and worked for a greeting card company before turning to book illustration. Today she lives near Peterborough, Ontario, and works in a studio at her home that offers wonderful views of the outdoors. She is a writer and illustrator and has collaborated with many artists, including her husband Henry and daughter Kim.

Ribbon Rescue is Eugenie's first book with Robert Munsch. It was important to her to reflect the energy and animation of Munsch's lively story in the illustrations. Before beginning the illustrations, she looked at the photographs that Robert Munsch provided of the real Jillian, her family, and her community. Many of the details in the illustrations — the cabin with the lacrosse sticks in front, the church in the village — are based on details in the photographs. Jillian herself, and of course the ribbon dress, are also drawn from real life. Eugenie enjoyed putting her imagination to work in creating lively illustrations to match the zaniness of the story. As she says, "It's always great to work with someone at the top! I'd do it again!"

... that Eugenie had hoped that the illustration of Jillian finding the ring in the pond would be used for the front cover of the book?
- Why do you think that picture was not chosen for the cover?
- Which picture would you pick for the cover illustration?

Take a look

Eugenie has loved nature, animals, and spending time outdoors since she was a child. How does she communicate that love in the illustrations for *Ribbon Rescue?* Hint: Follow the frogs and the cat in the story.

PLAYHOUSE

Dear Mr. Munsch,

My favourite part in play house is when Rene gets everthing she wants.

love your friend,
Kendall

Summary:

Rene lives in the country. She doesn't want to play with her younger brothers, so she asks her father to build her a playhouse. It's a great playhouse, almost like a real house — but not quite. She decorates it, and adds a play barn and some play animals, but it still doesn't feel quite right. It starts to feel right when she adds a play family — which, unlike a real family, isn't bossy or annoying. But when her real family creates a play Rene to replace her, Rene realizes that sometimes you need the real thing, even with all the trouble that goes with it!

Questions:

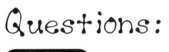

Before

Look at the front cover.
- Where do you think this story takes place?
- What is the key for?
- What do you notice about the lettering of the title?
- What does that tell you about the book?
- What is the equipment in the background of the cover illustration? Why do you think that might be at the farm?

Look at the back cover.
- What information can we find about the author and the illustrator?
- Read the description of the book on the back, and make some predictions to answer the "teaser."

Read the dedication page.
- Sometimes illustrators use an important image on the dedication page that tells us about the main idea of the story. Why might this illustration be here?

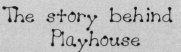

The story behind Playhouse

In 1996, Robert Munsch received a letter from Rene, who lives near Endeavour, Saskatchewan. She told him about her chores on the farm, and about the playhouse that her father built for her. He liked her letter so he wrote back and included a story he quickly made up about her playhouse. In 1999, he was travelling in Saskatchewan, so he asked if he could visit Rene and her family on their farm. They were glad to see him! They showed him the farm and he was very surprised to see that they lived in the middle of the woods, not in the middle of flat prairies. Rene's father had trunk cutters and tree snippers and log grabbers that he used in his work as a logger. Robert Munsch took many pictures of Rene's house and farm and all of the equipment. He gave the photographs to Michael Martchenko when he was illustrating *Playhouse*. Look at the illustrations and see if you can find the things that Robert Munsch found on Rene's farm.

- To whom did Robert Munsch dedicate this book? (Find Endeavour, Saskatchewan, on a map).
- How do you think he knows Rene?

During

Notice if your predictions were correct.
- p. 4: How is Rene's playhouse like a real house? How is it "not quite" like a real house?
- p. 14: She has a house, barn, animals; now what do you think she wants?
- p. 16: Why does she need all of the equipment around her playhouse?
- p. 18: How is Rene going to solve her problem? How is she going to get her play mommy and play daddy?
- p. 22: How does Rene feel about the play Rene?
- p. 29: Why does Rene get pictures of food?

After

- Why does Rene's mother make a play Rene?
- Why does Rene destroy her?
- Why do you think that the real things are better than the play ones in the end?
- Make a list of all the problems Rene solves through the story.
- How would you describe Rene?

Take a look

Make sure you give children the chance to examine and enjoy the illustrations. In this story children should notice . . .

🌀 the side story of the hens, rooster and fox told through the illustrations. They could write that story, and read more stories about hens and foxes such as *Rosie's Walk*, *Hattie and the Fox*, and *One Fine Day*.

🌀 the quirky details or things that "don't fit," such as the TV, satellite dish, and coffee can in the tractor; the gopher on the lounge chair; Rene reading a book to laughing hens, and much more.

The Real Rene and the Real Me

This activity gives students an opportunity to think about the character of Rene in more detail. As a class, complete a Character Cube for Rene and then have students complete cubes about themselves. Students could also be put in pairs to interview and complete cubes about each other as a "getting to know you" activity at the beginning of the year.

Curriculum Link:

Language Arts — interviewing, character analysis
Social Studies — personal identity, respect for others

Materials:

2 class sets of Character Cubes (see reproducible on p. 13)
(optional) Sheets of construction paper, 12" x 18"

Procedure:

1. Brainstorm with the class the things they know about Rene after reading *Playhouse*, and settle on five. Among other things, they may point out that:

◎ She is the oldest child in her family. She has two younger brothers.

◎ She has fish for pets.

◎ She is a good artist.

◎ She is a good problem-solver.

◎ She likes to play in her playhouse.

2. Create a set of five questions that you could ask Rene in an interview to encourage her to give you this information. Your interview questions might look like this:

◎ Who are the people in your family?

◎ Do you have any pets?

◎ What are you good at?

◎ What would someone else say you are good at?

◎ What do you do for fun?

3. Students could be placed in pairs to practise interviewing. One could be the interviewer and ask the questions you created. The other could be Rene and provide the answers you brainstormed.

4. Demonstrate to students how they are going to record the information they got about Rene from the book and your interview on a character cube. Each side of the cube should have the answer to one question and an illustration on it. (Note that a cube has six sides and they only have five questions. Suggest that the sixth side should include Rene's name and a picture of her.)

5. Once students have completed a character cube for Rene, they should complete another cube about themselves, answering the same questions you created for Rene. Alternatively, students could be placed in pairs to interview each other using the same questions. They could then create character cubes for their partners and after sharing them with the class, present them to their partners as gifts.

Extension:

◎ Use Venn diagrams to compare and contrast Rene and the students in your class.

PROCEED WITH CAUTION

Remember to be careful whenever you ask children about their families. Be sensitive to the variety of family settings represented by your students, and to the fact that some of them may not be living with their families.

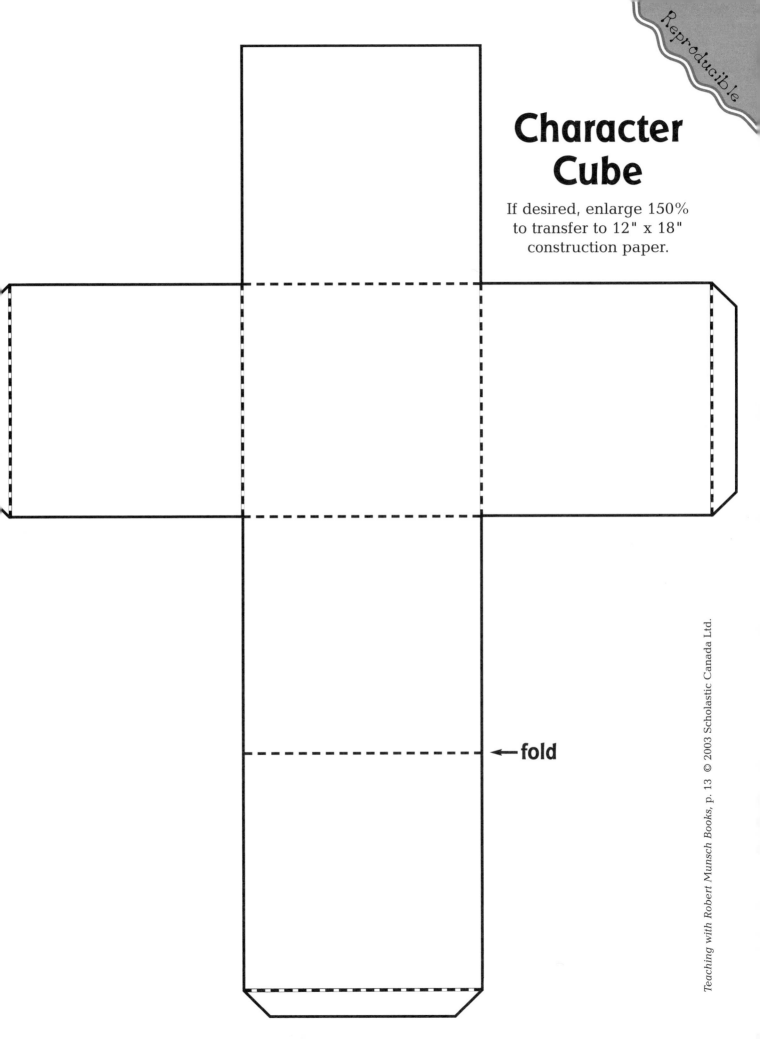

Character Cube

If desired, enlarge 150% to transfer to 12" x 18" construction paper.

←— **fold**

Teaching with Robert Munsch Books, p. 13 © 2003 Scholastic Canada Ltd.

Building a City Playhouse

In *Playhouse*, Rene creates a farm playhouse. In this activity, children will compare and contrast rural and urban environments, and build a model playhouse of their own.

Curriculum Link:
Social Studies — urban and rural environments
Science — building things
Math — 2-D and 3-D objects, measurement

Materials:
Plasticine, Popsicle sticks, stir sticks, pipe cleaners, milk cartons, cereal boxes, shoeboxes, paper towel rolls, toilet paper rolls

Procedure:
1. Remind students that *Playhouse* takes place on a farm. Quickly scan the illustrations again and ask students how they know Rene lives on a farm.

2. Tell students that Rene lives in a "rural" community, or in the country. Brainstorm other elements of life in a rural environment that do not appear in the book. Record students' answers on one side of a T-chart.

3. Once students have identified various characteristics of rural communities, brainstorm and record what they know about urban communities on the other side of the T-chart.

4. Ask them what an "urban," or city, playhouse would look like. Would it look the same as Rene's? What would be the same? What might be different?

5. Give students the opportunity to sketch their ultimate urban playhouse. Ask them to explain their sketches to the class.

6. Challenge students to build a model of a city playhouse. Incorporate math skills by requiring that students draw plans for their playhouse and include appropriate measurements. Allow students to use materials such as Plasticine, Popsicle sticks, stir sticks and pipe cleaners to fashion their playhouses. You could include lessons on 2-D and 3-D shapes by requiring that students incorporate various materials such as milk cartons, shoeboxes, and paper rolls into the design of their playhouses.

Extensions:

◎ Write journal entries about what a rural or urban playhouse would look like.

◎ Build language skills by asking students to act as "Playhouse Realtors" and write ads persuading people to buy their dream playhouse.

MAKEUP MESS

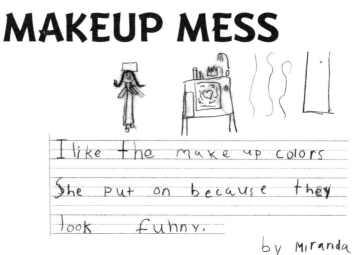

I like the make up colors
She put on because they
look funny.

by Miranda

Summary:

Julie uses all the money she has saved from her birthday, Christmas, and paper route to buy a huge box of makeup. After she returns from the drugstore, she covers her face in purple, green, and black makeup, colours her hair, and wears nineteen earrings in one ear and seventeen in the other. Julie thinks she looks beautiful, but her parents don't seem to agree.

Questions:

Before

Look at the front cover.
- What do you notice about the lettering used in the title?
- Who do you think the two younger children might be?

Look at the back cover.
- What information can we find out about the author? the illustrator?
- Who is the child in this book?
- Read the description on the back, and predict why you think Julie's parents were not pleased with her makeup.
- Record the students' predictions on a chart.

During

- p. 2: How old do you think Julie might be? Look for clues in the picture to help you.
- p. 4: Why do you think Julie would want to wear makeup?
- p. 11: What do you think the two younger children might be thinking?

- p. 12: Why are Julie's parents acting strange?
- p. 16: Who do you think might be at the door?
- p. 26: How much money would Julie make from selling the makeup?

After

- Check the chart for students' predictions.
- Why did Julie sell her makeup at the end of the story?
- Suggest to the students that they write their own story entitled "Dress-up Mess."

by Kelsey

Once there was a girl named Julia. She was watching her sister Jana play dress up. She thought if Jana could wear dresses then she could wear dresses so she saved up three hundred dollars and she went to town and bought three hundred dresses and
(1)

she looked in the mirror and she said I look BEAUTIFUL! and her mom said AAAAAA! and she went to go see her dad and he said AAAAA!
(2)

Then she wore a yellow and green and grey dress and she looked in the mirror and she said I look BEAUTIFUL and the mail man came to the door and she said I better go show the mailman
(3)

and the mailman said AAAAAA. and she said in think I want to go back to my normal self. So she gave all her dressup mess away and she went to go show her mom her dad and the mailman and they said you look BEAUTIFUL and she went to look in the mirror and she said I do look nice and she said I know some thing better Shoes!!
(4)

Take a look

- What is out of place on page 16 and 17?

- How many of Robert Munsch's books, or references to his books, can you find in the illustrations throughout the story?

- Point out the name of the drugstore on p. 7.

Spending Munsch Money

In this activity, the students will be working with larger denominations of money — 5, 10 and 20 dollars. They will have the opportunity to add larger numbers and to make change. This activity also provides time for the teacher to informally observe the children as they are working in pairs, and to assess their understanding of money.

Curriculum Link:
Math — money, adding larger numbers

Materials:
Enough bins for students to work in pairs
Small objects, e.g. pencils, stickers, erasers, small toys
Labels for price tags
$100 of Munsch Money for each group (see reproducible on p. 20)
Bills (see reproducible on p. 21)

Preparation:
Price the items ahead of time. You may want to have the children help you determine the prices.

Procedure:

1. Begin by discussing with the children their experiences with money. Do you get an allowance? Have you spent money at the store? Have you ever saved your money to buy something special?

2. Look back at page 2 in the story, and point out to the students that Julie had collected $100. Explain to the students that they are going to have the opportunity to do some buying and selling using "Munsch money" in their own store.

3. Divide the students into pairs and give each pair a bin with the items you have priced, the Munsch money and the bills. Explain to the children that they are going to take turns being the storekeeper and the customer.

4. You may want to model this activity with the whole group before they begin working in pairs. For example, invite a volunteer to be the storekeeper and another volunteer to be the customer. Have the customer choose two items to buy. The storekeeper will write a bill for the customer, adding the two items together. The customer will then pay the storekeeper the appropriate amount using his or her Munsch money.

5. For students who need more of a challenge, you might suggest that they buy three items at a time. You might also encourage the customer to give the storekeeper an amount that would involve getting change back. They could also try to find as many different ways as they can to spend the $100.

Extension:
◎ Read other books about spending money, such as *Alexander, Who Used to Be Rich Last Sunday*; *Pigs Will Be Pigs*; and *A Bargain for Frances.*

Munsch Money

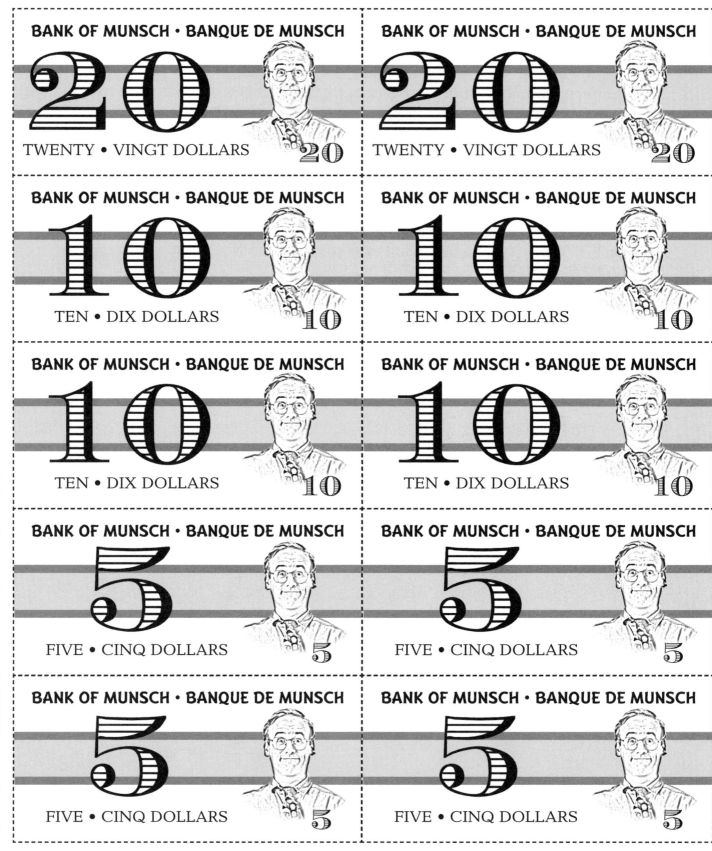

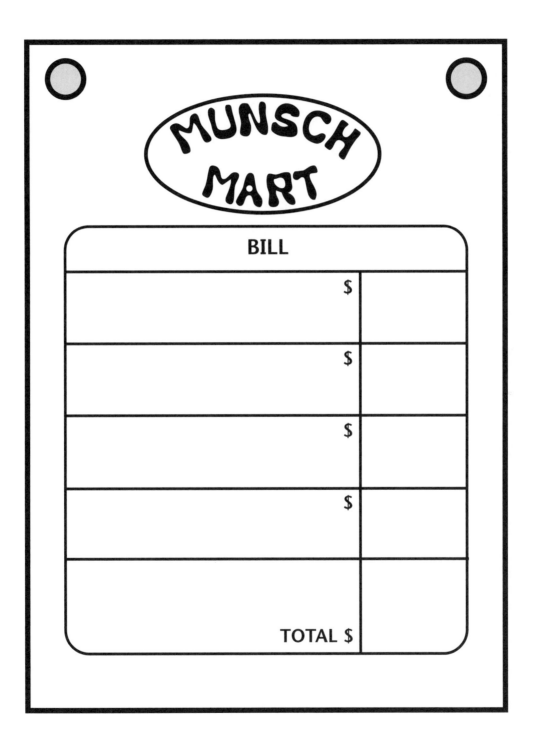

MUNSCH MART

BILL

	$	
	$	
	$	
	$	
TOTAL $		

Friendship Circle

It is important for children to know that they and others around them are unique and beautiful in their own way. They all make valuable and differing contributions to the classroom community. This activity will allow the children to reflect on who they are and the qualities that make them beautiful — inside and out.

Curriculum Link:

Language Arts — descriptive listmaking
Social Studies — personal identity, respecting others and strengthening community, working within groups
Art — observation, creativity, fine motor skills

Materials:

Character Webs (see reproducible on p. 24)
Class set of Body Shapes (see reproducible on p. 25)
Scraps of fabric, coloured yarn, construction paper, plastic eyes, scissors, glue

Procedure:

1. Divide the students into pairs and ask them to think about the special characteristics of their partner.

2. Using the reproducible, have the students create character webs of each other, by listing the traits that they think make the other person special. When the webs are completed, they might like to share them with the whole group.

3. Reread page 24 of *Makeup Mess* to the students. What happened that made Julie realize that she didn't need makeup to look beautiful?
Discuss with the students how we are all special, beautiful, and unique individuals.

4. Each of us has special talents and interests that we can share with others. Invite the students to use the reproducible template to make a paper model of themselves. Provide them with a variety of materials, e.g. scraps of fabric, construction paper, coloured yarn, coloured tissue, plastic eyes.

5. Once the students have completed their self-images, arrange them in a circle or a line on a bulletin board so that their hands are touching. In the centre of the display you might want to put the caption, "Friendship Circle" or "Our Classroom Community." Near each image, attach the character web for that person.

Extension:

◎ You could select a "Special Person of the Week." Each student in the class could write something special about this person and draw a picture of him or her. These could be compiled into a book for the Special Person to take home.

Character Web

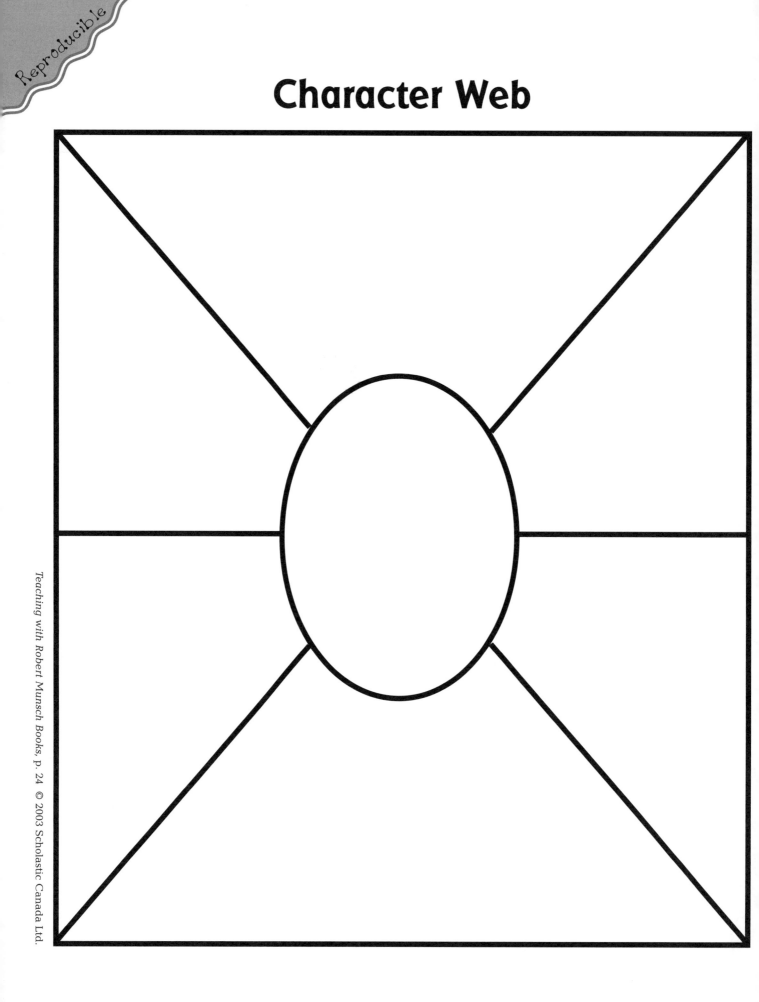

Teaching with Robert Munsch Books, p. 24 © 2003 Scholastic Canada Ltd.

Body Shape

Teaching with Robert Munsch Books, p. 25 © 2003 Scholastic Canada Ltd.

This is the only Robert Munsch story ever published that is based on an idea sent to him by a parent. In 1995, Amy's mother wrote to Robert Munsch and told him how difficult it was to wake Amy up every morning. One morning, Amy refused to get out of bed, and her mother suggested that maybe they should take her to school in her bed. Amy thought that was hilarious, and both she and her mother thought it was a terrific idea for a book, a Robert Munsch book to be exact. Robert Munsch thought it was a good story idea too, so he wrote a draft and put it in his special binder. In 1998, an editor found the story and suggested that he turn it into a book. When the people in Amy's home town, Tavistock, Ontario, found out that Robert Munsch was writing a book about her, they invited him to their fall fair to celebrate the book's launch. He and Amy rode on a special float, complete with her bed and about twenty friends!

GET OUT OF BED!

Dear Robert Munsch,

How are you doing? My favourite Book that you wrote is Get out of Bed because it is funny. Which book is your favourite?

From _____

Dylan _____

Summary:

Amy stays up very late at night watching television. This means that she is so sleepy she doesn't get out of bed in the mornings. One morning, no one in Amy's family can wake her up. They decide to take her to school in her bed. She sleeps through the entire school day and the evening, and does not wake up until the next morning. At school the next day, she discovers that everyone in her class has decided that sleeping at school looks like fun.

Questions:

Before

Look at the front cover.
- Notice that different illustrators have worked with Robert Munsch.
- How does this book look the same or different from other Munsch books you have read?

Look at the back cover.
- What information can we find about the author and the illustrators?
- Read the description of the book on the back and predict how Amy's brother solves her problem.
- Record students' predictions on a chart.

Look at the title page.
- Where are these two boys?
- Read the dedication page.
- To whom did Robert Munsch dedicate this book? (Find Tavistock, Ontario, on a map.) How do you think he knows Amy?

During

- p. 6: What will Amy's father do to wake her up?
- p. 9: What is Amy's mother going to do?
- p. 12: Check the chart for students' predictions.
- p. 21: Is Amy going to wake up before home time?
- p. 27: What did everyone do?
- p. 30: What time is it? What are Amy and her brother doing?

After

- Why were all the children in the classroom sleeping?
- Look at the title page again, and discuss how the illustration gave them a clue as to what was going to happen.
- Look at the last illustration again: What do you think is going to happen the next day?

Take a look

Alan and Lea Daniel, like many of Robert Munsch's illustrators, enjoy adding animals to the story. In fact, in this story, Amy's pets appear in every spread but one. Find the picture that doesn't actually show the pets. Where do you think they are hiding?

Compare and contrast the Daniels' illustrations with those of Robert Munsch's other illustrators. Look at some books these illustrators have done with other authors. Do Munsch's stories seem to suggest a certain kind of illustration?

Solving Problems

This activity gives students an opportunity to think about some typical problems every household faces: sharing chores and sharing toys. It also introduces a specific problem-solving strategy that may be applied to many areas of their family and school lives, and to other curriculum areas.

Curriculum Link:
Social Studies — problem-solving, conflict resolution, family responsibilities

Materials:
Two class sets of the Decision Tree (see reproducible on p. 30)

Procedure:

1. Distribute the Decision Tree reproducible, and then lead the class through the problem-solving process.

2. Identify the problem Amy's family had at the beginning of the story, i.e., Amy would not get out of bed in the morning.

3. Fill in one side of the Decision Tree with the solution the family came up with (taking Amy to school in her bed), and the consequences of that decision.

4. With the children, brainstorm other solutions the family might have tried. Choose one of the solutions suggested, and fill in the other side of the Decision Tree with that solution and a consequence that might result.

5. Ask the children to complete the Decision Tree by identifying the better solution. They should be prepared to defend their choice.

6. Distribute blank copies of the Decision Tree.

7. Brainstorm other family and school issues that students could practise solving. Use picture books to generate some ideas if necessary. Good choices include:

- *Really, Really* — in which a girl lies to her babysitter about snacks, bedtime, and other family expectations

- *When Mom Turned Into a Monster* — about a mother who literally turns into a monster when she doesn't get any help with the chores

- *The Recess Queen* — about a girl who comes to a new school and meets a playground bully

8. Let students work in pairs to identify the problem, two possible solutions, and their consequences. Ask them to choose the better solution, and then share their problems with the class.

Extension:

- Students can role-play the problems and solutions they worked out.

- Students can write, or illustrate a picture, about a time they solved a family or school problem.

- Students can write letters describing a problem and asking for advice. Other students can write back with suggestions for ways to solve the problem.

Decision Tree

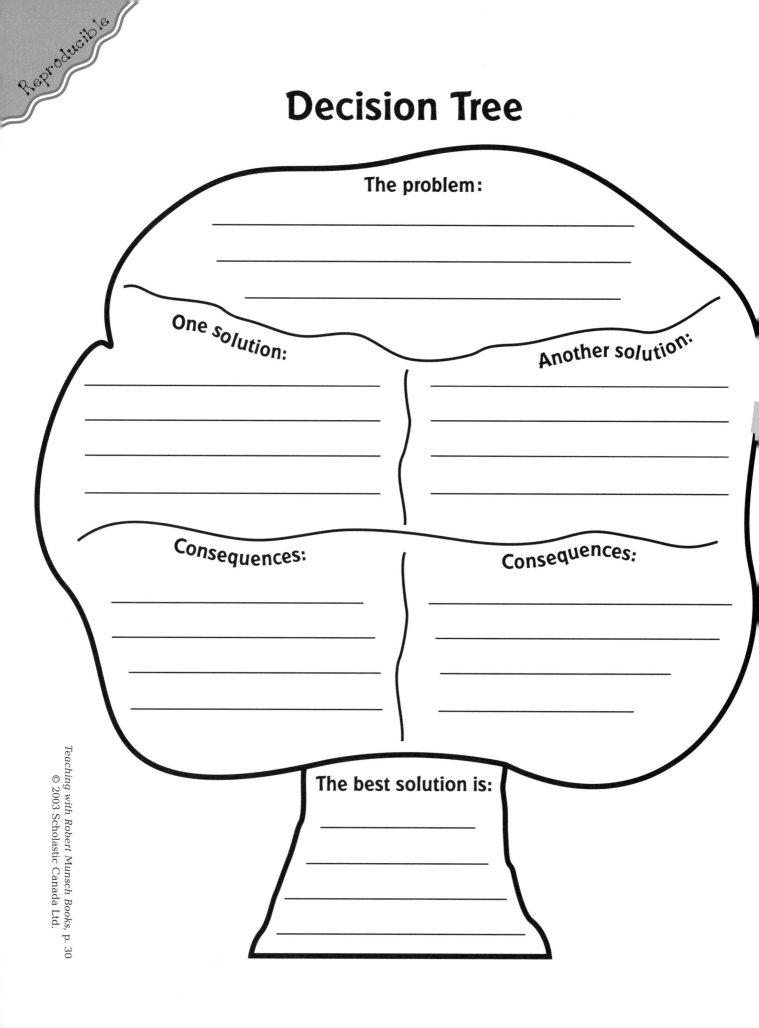

The problem:

_____

_____

_____

One solution:

_____

_____

_____

_____

Another solution:

_____

_____

_____

Consequences:

_____

_____

_____

Consequences:

_____

_____

_____

The best solution is:

_____

_____

_____

_____

Teaching with Robert Munsch Books, p. 30
© 2003 Scholastic Canada Ltd.

Just in Time

Central to the development of historical understanding in young children is an understanding of time concepts and of the sequencing of events. These events do not need to be important historical events; young children simply need to practise placing the events of their own days — or lives — in chronological order.

Curriculum Link:
Social Studies — time and continuity
Math — time, sequence

Materials:
Chart or pocket chart
Events from story written on large cards
Analog clock
Digital clock
Class set of A Day in the Life reproducible (see p. 33)

Procedure:

1. Write the following events from the story on large cards and place them at random on the board: "Breakfast," "Reading Lesson," "Dinner," "Art Lesson," "Recess."

2. On chart paper or in a pocket chart, place the first event in the story: "Amy watches TV." Write "4 a.m." beside it, showing what that time would look like on an analog and on a digital clock.

3. Ask the students to place the events you have identified on large cards in the order in which they happened in the story. (Leave space between each event.)

4. Estimate what time these events might have happened. Write these times beside the events, showing what that time would look like on an analog and on a digital clock.

5. Identify other events from the story, such as arriving at school and gym class, and place them in the appropriate places in the chart. Identify events that would probably happen in Amy's day but that don't appear in the story, such as bedtime, and place them in the appropriate places in the chart. Again, identify logical times for these events.

6. Distribute copies of A Day in the Life.

7. Have students identify six events in their typical day. Their lists might include breakfast, arriving at school, math class, lunch, piano lesson, bedtime. Ask them to place these events in sequence and indicate on the blank clock faces what time these events take place.

Extensions:

◎ Take photos of events during the course of the day in the classroom. Ask students to use clues in the photos to place them in chronological order.

◎ Make paper-plate clocks that students could use to sequence events of a day. The book *Time To . . .* is a useful demonstration of this. Students could use their clocks to solve word problems such as, "Reading class starts at 9:00 a.m. and is forty minutes long. What time does reading class end?"

◎ Make a timeline of photographs or illustrations of important events during the course of the school year.

A Day in the Life

Time	Event
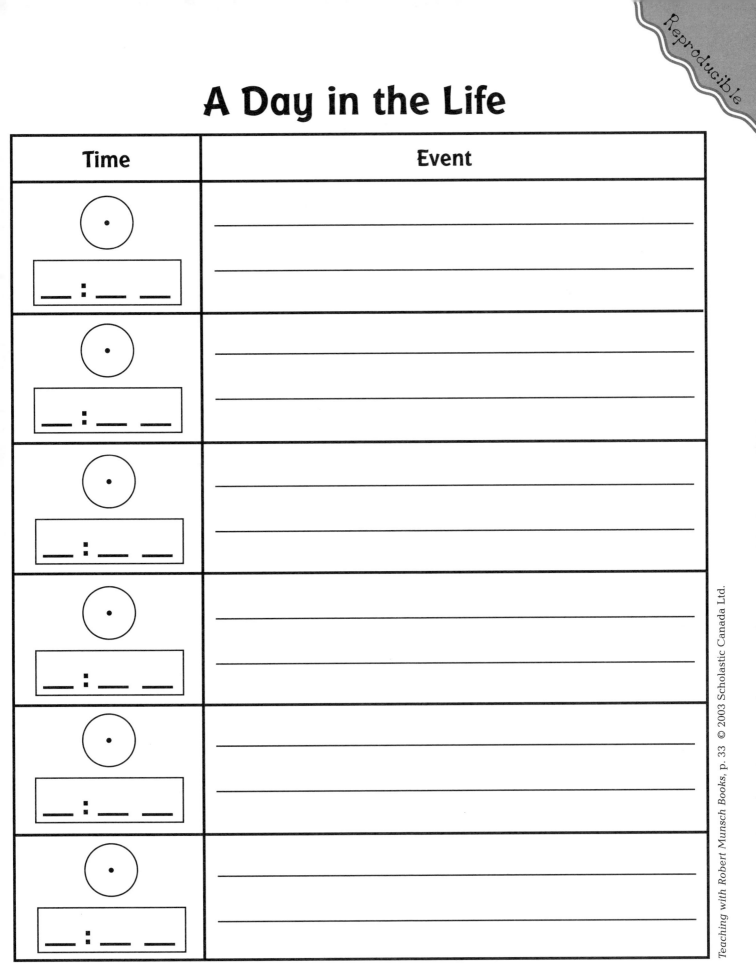	

The story behind
Alligator Baby

On Kristen's birthday in 1979, Robert Munsch made up a story for her. He knew her mother was going to have a baby, so he told a funny story about how Kristen's parents went to the zoo instead of the hospital and brought back the wrong baby. Kristen was so happy with the story that she wrote it down and drew illustrations for it. When Robert Munsch asked her if she would still like to be the girl in the story when he was ready to publish it many years later, she showed him her version of the book. In 1997, she received Robert Munsch's and Michael Martchenko's version to add to her library, and so did we!

ALLIGATOR BABY

Q: "Are you going to release a continuation to *Alligator Baby*?"
Rachel, Grade 4
"P.S. I really like your books."

A: "I don't have a continuation of *Alligator Baby*, not even in my head. Do you have an idea for a continuation?"
Robert Munsch

Summary:

Kristen's mother is having a baby! On the way to the hospital, her parents get lost and end up at the city zoo. When her mother and father arrive home, they discover that they have the wrong baby. They have come home with an alligator baby. Through a series of hilarious events, Kristen eventually brings her baby brother home.

Questions:

Before

Look at the front cover.
- Why do you think the mother is holding a baby alligator?
- Where did this alligator come from?
- What do you notice about the lettering used in the title? What does this tell you about the book?

Look at the back cover.
- Read the description on the back of the book, and predict where Kristen's real baby brother is and how she will get him back. Record students' predictions on a chart.

Read the dedication page.
- To whom did Robert Munsch dedicate this book? (Find Guelph, Ontario, on a map.) How do you think he knows Kristen?

During

- p. 9:   What will they find under the blanket this time?
- p. 15: Look at the feet sticking out of the blanket. What animal has
  Kristen's mother brought home this time?
- p. 16: What is Kristen going to do?
- p. 20: How is Kristen going to get her baby brother from the gorilla?
- p. 26: What do you think Kristen sees out the window?

After

- Check the predictions you made before reading the book.
- How did the animals know where to find their babies?
- What do you think happened when Kristen's mother had twins?
- The children could write their own story describing what happens next.

Research Project

In this activity, students will have the opportunity to research some of the animals featured in the book. If this is the students' first experience with research, you may want to begin as a class project, using specific categories and recording key facts and ideas as a group. This project may span over a two- to three-week period.

Curriculum Link:
Language arts — developing research skills
Science — needs of animals, animal life cycles

Materials:
Class set of Research Webs (see reproducible on p. 38-39)
Information books: see List of Resources (p. 59) for suggestions

Procedure:

1. Select one of the animals in the story to further explore through a research project. With the students, brainstorm questions they may have about this animal and record them on chart paper for future reference. Look at the questions and divide them into categories e.g. food, habitat, enemies, protection, description, and interesting facts.

2. You may want to focus on one category at a time. Share the information books with the students, on the category you have selected to research that day. You may also want to make the books available for the students to read during their independent reading time.

3. Provide the students with a Research Web each, and have them fill in the section you have discussed, using point form. You may want to do this together on the overhead, or demonstrate one on a chart. This is also a wonderful opportunity to talk to the students about the purpose of using point form to gather information.

4. Once their webs are completed, demonstrate for the students how to write up the information from their webs into paragraphs.

5. Each student can than staple the completed paragraphs into a shape booklet of the animal he or she has researched.

6. Invite the students to illustrate their reports.

Extensions:

◎ Students could select a second animal to research — as a class, with a partner or individually. You could then compare and contrast this animal with the first one selected.

◎ Ask the students to prepare a short speech explaining why they would like to have this animal for a baby brother or sister.

Research Web

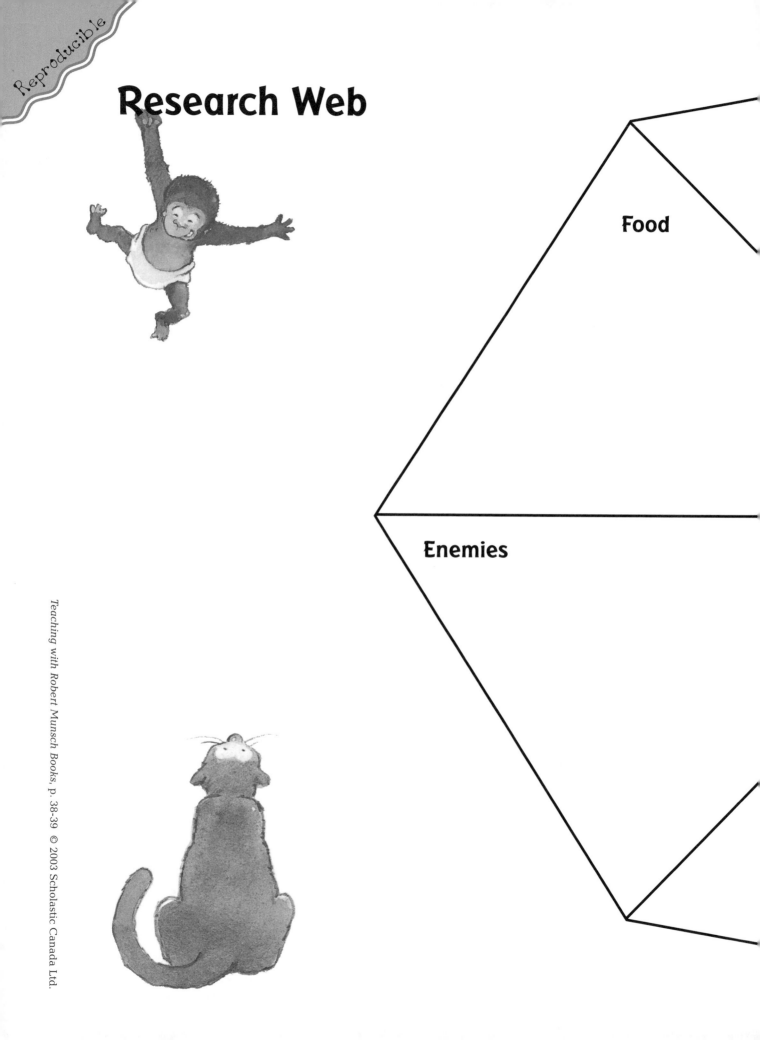

Food

Enemies

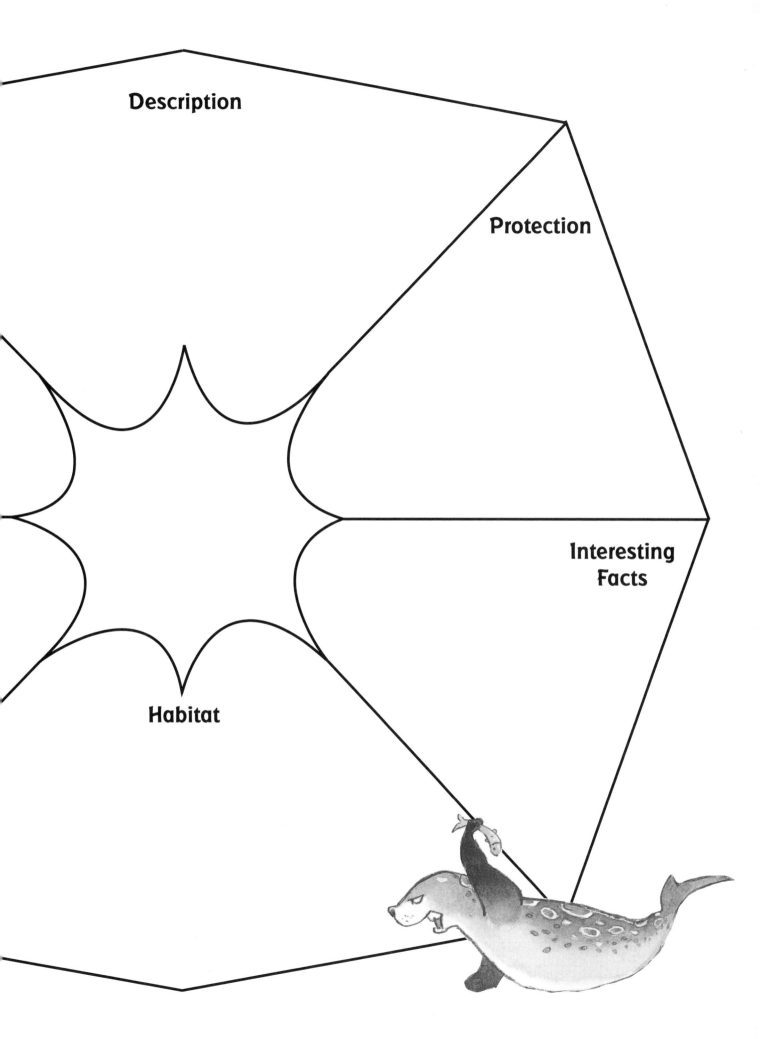

Description

Protection

Interesting Facts

Habitat

Write a Riddle

In this activity, the students can use the information they have researched from activity #1 to create their own animal riddles.

Curriculum Links:
Language Arts — descriptive listmaking
Science — animal characteristics

Materials:
Coloured construction paper
Large white index cards (4 per student)
Riddle books — 6 sheets of 9" x 12" coloured construction paper stapled together (these may be prepared ahead of time by a volunteer)

Procedure:

1. Explain to the students that they are going to create their own riddle books using the different animals featured in the story.

2. Begin by sharing examples of riddles with the students — from books, or some that you have created.

3. Look back at the description of the alligator on page 4: "a long green tail," "a long green face with lots of teeth." Together, write a riddle for an alligator using four clues and ending with "Who am I?" If you selected alligators as one of the animals to research in activity #1, you may want to refer back to the information you gathered, or gather ideas by sharing information books about alligators with the students.

4. As a way of introducing the riddle books, have each student write one riddle for practice. Fold a piece of 9" x 12" construction paper in half. Glue the riddle on the top flap. Inside the flap, have each student illustrate the answer to the riddle. Share these riddles in the Author's Chair.

5. Before the children begin their own riddle books, have them select the four animals that will be featured in their books. Have the students do a first draft of their riddles for you to revise and edit. Once the riddles have been edited, the students can copy their riddles onto index cards, which will be glued into their riddle books.

6. Have the students glue their riddles on the left-hand side of the page and illustrate the animal on the right-hand side of the page. The students can glue a flap over the illustration to hide their answer. The children could share their riddle books with their classmates and with other classes in the school.

Extensions:

◎ You could use a pop-up riddle format for the books.

◎ Students could write an acrostic poem about one of their favourite animals in the story.

◎ Share a variety of chants, poems, and songs about the different animals.

Robert Munsch told many versions of *We Share Everything!* for several years. The children at the schools and daycares where he told these stories liked them, even though he didn't think they were very good. Then one day in 1992, while he was telling the story in his daughter Tyya's Grade 1 class, he used the line, "This is kindergarten. In kindergarten we share!" The children loved this line, and joined in whenever it came up in the story. Now he thought he was onto something! He kept telling the story, improving parts of it every time. In 1998, he decided to turn it into a book, but he didn't really have any specific children in mind to feature. He found the children on a visit to a class in Pontiac, Michigan. Amanda and Jeremiah wanted to be in the story, and they loved to share!

WE SHARE EVERYTHING!

Q: "How long did it take you to write *We Share Everything!?*"
Jessica, Grade 3

A: "It took me six years to get it right!"
Robert Munsch .... slow!

Summary:

On the first day of kindergarten, Amanda and Jeremiah fight about books, blocks and paints. The teacher reminds them that in kindergarten, they should share everything. Amanda and Jeremiah interpret her message literally, and share their clothes with each other.

Questions:

Before

Look at the front cover.
- Where are the children?
- What is the book in the illustration?

Look at the back cover.
- What information can we find about the author and the illustrator?

Read the dedication page.
- Who are Amanda and Jeremiah?
- Where is Pontiac, Michigan?

During

- p. 10: Will Amanda give him the book?
- p. 15: Why would the illustrator draw birds and flowers around the teacher?
- p. 16: What is going to happen next?
- p. 26: What else are they going to share?

- What might your parents say if you came home wearing different clothes?
- What problems did Amanda and Jeremiah have? How might they have solved their problems?

Take a look

How many of Robert Munsch's books can you find in the illustrations?

Sharing Rules!

Amanda and Jeremiah's antics in *We Share Everything!* provide an amusing demonstration of inappropriate classroom behaviour. This activity gives children an opportunity to explore the reasons why we share in school, the kinds of things we share, and why it is important to have rules.

Curriculum Link:

Language Arts — effective story-writing tools, listmaking
Social Studies — classroom rules and responsibilities
Art — promotional art

Materials:

Large paper
Coloured pencils or felt pens

Procedure:

1. Discuss what makes this story funny. Emphasize that Robert Munsch stories are often funny because he exaggerates or writes about things that are too ridiculous to ever happen. For example, children in class would not actually exchange their clothes.

2. Discuss what kinds of things we would share in a classroom (supplies, toys at centres) and what kinds of things we would not share (personal items).

3. Note that when they didn't share, Amanda and Jeremiah argued and did things that were unsafe. Discuss how the rest of the children in their class must have felt.

4. Explain that in order to avoid these situations, we have class rules. Brainstorm rules that the class should have and list them on chart paper. (Add some visual cues if necessary).

5. Ask students to choose one rule and illustrate it. They could be provided with a caption or write their own if appropriate.

Extensions:

◎ Students can draw a picture of Amanda and Jeremiah cooperating and sharing in their kindergarten class.

◎ Students could use magazines and other materials to make a collage about sharing.

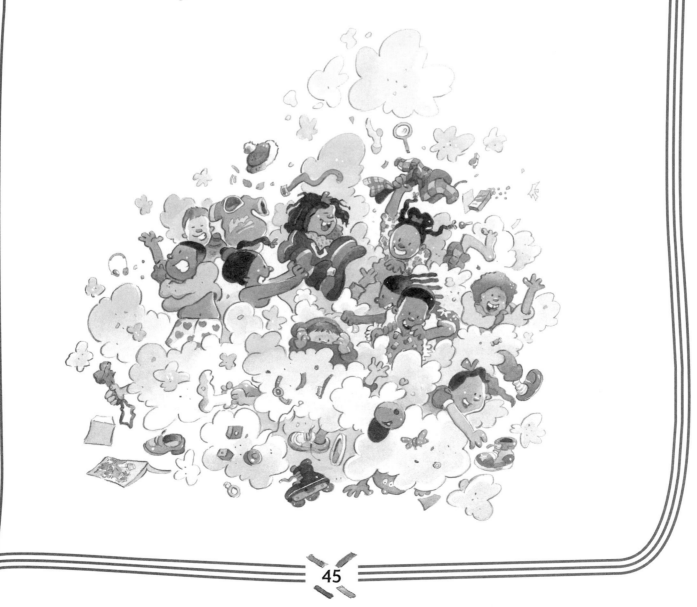

Building Monuments

Jeremiah builds some impressive structures with the blocks in the kindergarten class. Challenge students to build some other important world landmarks at the block centre.

Curriculum Link:
Social Studies — geography
Science — building things

Materials:
Pictures of the Eiffel Tower and
   Notre Dame Cathedral in Paris
Pictures of other global landmarks
   (*World Famous Landmarks* has
   some useful suggestions)
Blocks
Atlas for young children

Procedure:

1. Show the children photographs of the Eiffel Tower and Notre Dame Cathedral in Paris. Compare the photographs to the illustrations of Jeremiah's block creations on pages 17 and 32. You might want to note Jeremiah's beret on page 17 and locate Paris, France, on a map of the world. You might also want to share other picture books set in Paris that feature these landmarks, like Ludwig Bemelmans' *Madeline.*

2. Share some other photographs of important landmarks, natural or manmade, around the world or around your community. Children could share information about places they have visited or landmarks they have seen.

3. Leave the photographs at the block centre and give children the opportunity to build various landmarks. You could challenge them to use specific shapes of blocks to create specific landmarks such as the Great Pyramid in Egypt, Prince Edward Island's Confederation Bridge or the Parliament Buildings in Ottawa.

Extension:

◎ Ask students to mark the locations of their landmarks on a map of the world that can be left at the block centre.

RIBBON RESCUE

Q: "When I read your book *Ribbon Rescue* I really liked it when she was helping all of the other people."
Kelsey, Grade 3

A: "Thank you. The real Jillian would do something like that, because she likes to help people."
Robert Munsch

Summary:

Jillian's grandmother makes her a beautiful traditional Mohawk ribbon dress. While Jillian is outside admiring her new dress, a bride and groom and a group of frantic wedding guests race by on their way to the church, exclaiming that they are lost and going to be late. Jillian helps each one by sharing the ribbons from her dress to fix their problems. Unfortunately, Jillian ends up being a mess, and risks missing the wedding herself.

Questions:

Before

Look at the front cover.
- What do you think the title *Ribbon Rescue* might mean?
- What do you notice about the lettering used in the title?
- Where do you think everyone is going in such a hurry? Record the students' predictions on a chart.

Look at the back cover.
- Note: Omit reading the story description, and consider having the students write their own blurb after you have read the story.
- Share the information about the author and illustrator.

Read the dedication page.
- Find Kahnawake, Quebec, on the map and explain to the students that this is a Mohawk reserve.

During

- p. 2: Explain to the students that this is a traditional Mohawk dress that Jillian's grandmother has made for her. Ask the students if they can find any other aboriginal symbols on the page. How many ribbons does Jillian's dress have?
- p. 6: How many ribbons does Jillian's dress have now? As you read the story, you might want to keep a tally on a chart of each time she gives a ribbon away.
- p. 9: Now how many ribbons does Jillian have left?
- p. 13: Check the chart for the students' predictions of where the people were going. At this point, what is the total number of ribbons Jillian has given away? How many ribbons does she have left?
- p. 25: What do you think will happen to Jillian now?

After

- Why did the author call this story *Ribbon Rescue?*
- Pretend there are more ribbons on the dress, and brainstorm other problems and solutions for Jillian.
- Try to find out more information about the Kahnawake reserve and Mohawk traditions to share with the students.
- Find out about other forms of traditional aboriginal clothing, and compare them to the Mohawk ribbon dress.

Take a look

- Are there clues in the illustrations that might make you think you are on a reserve?

- Looking at the illustrations, do you think this story takes place in the city or the country?

Activity #1

Class Survey

In this activity, students will have the opportunity to collect and present data through a class survey. Once the data has been organized into a bar graph, the students can compare their findings with each other.

Curriculum Link:
Math — data analysis

Materials:
Class set of Survey Charts (see reproducible on p. 52)
Class set of Bar Graphs (see reproducible on p. 53)

Procedure:

1. Begin by informing the students that there are a number of ways to collect data, and that today they are going to use the method of taking a survey. Explain to the students that a survey is a way of finding out information by asking people questions.

2. Refer back to the different methods of transportation that the bride and groom and guests used in the story to get to the church on time, i.e. skateboard, bicycle, scooter, in-line skates, and a wagon.

3. Invite the students to participate in a class survey. Have the students brainstorm ideas for different questions that they could ask their classmates, using the transportation items from the story. For example:
Which one is your favourite?
Which do you think would be the quickest way to get to the church?
Which one of these can you ride the best?

4. Talk to the students about how they will record their findings, i.e. tally marks, check marks, pictures.

5. Once each student has selected a question, have them all write their question at the top of their survey chart. Provide each student with a class list to help them keep track of which students they have surveyed. This will prevent asking the same person twice.

6. When the students have completed their surveys, have them share some of their findings with the rest of the class. Using one of the surveys as a sample, demonstrate for the students how they can now organize their data into a bar graph. You may also want to brainstorm with the students other ways of organizing the data.

7. Once the bar graphs are completed, ask questions such as: What is the most popular form of transportation? What is the least popular? How many more people preferred scooters to bicycles?

8. The students could write about this experience in their math journal, describing how they carried out the survey and what they learned about their classmates.

Name: _____

Survey Chart

Question: _____ _____ _____	
Scooter	
Bicycle	
Skateboard	
In-line skates	
Wagon	

Name: _____

Bar Graph

Scooter	Bicycle	Skateboard	In-line skates	Wagon

Mural Map

This activity will provide children with an opportunity to develop their mapping skills.

Curriculum Link:
Social Studies — mapping skills

Materials:
Large mural paper
Reproducible templates of objects found in the story
Paints, coloured pencils, scissors, glue

Procedure:

1. Begin by discussing with the students their experiences with maps. You may want to bring in some samples of different kinds of maps to share with the children. Ask questions such as: What is a map? What are maps used for? What different kinds of maps have you seen?

2. Explain to the students that they are going to create a mural map showing the route from Jillian's house to the church.

3. Brainstorm with the children the different landmarks they see along the way, e.g. storage shed, pond, trees, and houses, and record these on chart paper. Show the students how to place Jillian's house at one end of the mural paper, and the church at the other end.

4. Divide the students into pairs, and have them design their own mural maps of the route from Jillian's house to the church. The students can use the reproducible templates, and add landmarks not included on the master.

5. Once the maps are completed, have each group share their map. Compare and contrast the maps to see the similarities and differences.

Extension:

◎ Other great stories to map include *Hurry Up, Franklin!*, *The Gingerbread Boy*, and *We're Going on a Bear Hunt*.

Landmark Templates

Enlarge templates to suit classroom use.

Jillian's house

Storage shed

Pond

Woods

Church

Ideas for a Munsch Author Study

- Write and perform a readers' theatre production of your favourite Munsch book. Note: *Ribbon Rescue* works well.

- Make a puppet show with your favourite Munsch book.

- Design a book jacket of your favourite Robert Munsch book. The jackets could be laminated and displayed in a Munsch Corner in the classroom.

- Create a bookmark representing your favourite Munsch book. Choose a shape that reflects a character, building, or object in the book.

- Make character sketches for major characters in the Munsch books. What qualities do many of the main characters have in common?

- Use a shoebox or cardboard box to create a diorama of a scene from your favourite Robert Munsch book. Write a brief description about the book it came from, and which scene it represents. The dioramas and descriptions could be displayed in a glass case in the school.

- Create a Story Wheel of your favourite Robert Munsch book. Divide a circle into six to eight segments. Retell events of the story by moving clockwise around the circle.

- Make a Munsch Monument. Build a 3-D tribute to Munsch and include objects to represent the people or situations in his books. Explain what you included and why.

- Work with a partner to plan and create a mural of your favourite Robert Munsch book.

The mural could centre on the events of a particular Robert Munsch book, or it could be a mural representing your favourite Munsch characters. Use a variety of media to create your mural. For example: paints, chalk, pastels, construction paper, cotton balls, pipe cleaners, coloured tissue, scraps of material.

- Have a special lunch and come as your favourite Munsch character. Call it A Meal for Munschkins. Remember to have cookies and pies for dessert!

- Write a story in the style of Robert Munsch. Remember to include your favourite sound effects. (Check Robert Munsch's website for some examples from other classes).

- Write a letter to Robert Munsch applying for a job as his assistant. Tell him why you would be a great candidate to help him do his job.

- Many of Munsch's stories are outlandish or crazy. Create your own crazy stories by brainstorming possible characters (names of people, animals, aliens), settings (the zoo, barnyard, home), and problems (running out of food, making too much noise) for stories. Have students write each character, setting, and problem idea they come up with on a separate slip of paper. Collect all the slips in three bags marked "Characters," "Setting," and "Problem." Pairs of students can then choose several slips from the character bag, one from the setting bag, and one from the problem bag. Ask them to work together to write a story using the characters and setting they drew, and resolving the problem they chose.

- Compare and contrast the zany Munsch books with some of his more serious books, like *Love You Forever, From Far Away,* and *Lighthouse.*

- Listen to some of the stories on Robert Munsch's website. Are the stories he tells exactly the same as the stories in the books? Why or why not? What makes Robert Munsch such an effective storyteller? Practise retelling your favourite Munsch story.

- Many children and school classes write to Robert Munsch and try to convince him to come and visit. Look at some of the examples on his website, and then write your own letters and invitations trying to convince Robert Munsch to come for a visit.

- Make a commercial for a Munsch book. Write newspaper reviews of your favourite Munsch stories.

- After reading and responding to many Munsch books, ask students to consider why so many children enjoy Robert Munsch's stories. What do they expect when they prepare to listen to a Munsch story?

- Compare the books with some of the videos that have been made of Robert Munsch's stories.

- Invite parents or another class to a Munsch celebration. Children can read their favourite Munsch stories to parents or younger students, or even tell their favourite stories aloud.

- A class at Denne Elementary School in Newmarket, Ontario, got dressed up and held their own class awards show. Have your class do the same, and give out Munschie Awards for:
  - Best Major Character
  - Best Animal Character
  - Funniest Story
  - Best Illustrations
  - Favourite Story

LIST OF RESOURCES

Books by Robert Munsch

50 Below Zero
Aaron's Hair
Alligator Baby
Andrew's Loose Tooth
Angela's Airplane
Boy in the Drawer, The
Dark, The
David's Father
Fire Station, The
From Far Away
Get Me Another One
Get Out of Bed!
Giant
Good Families Don't
I Have to Go!
Jonathan Cleaned Up – Then He Heard a Sound
Lighthouse
Love You Forever
Makeup Mess
Millicent and the Wind
Mmm, Cookies!
Moira's Birthday
More Pies!
Mortimer
Mud Puddle
Munschworks
Munschworks 2
Munschworks 3
Munschworks 4
Munschworks Grand Treasury, The
Murmel, Murmel, Murmel
Paper Bag Princess, The
Pigs
Playhouse
Promise Is a Promise, A
Purple, Green and Yellow
Ribbon Rescue
Show and Tell
Something Good
Stephanie's Ponytail
Thomas' Snowsuit
Up, Up, Down
Wait and See
We Share Everything!
Where Is Gah-Ning?
Zoom!

Related Books

Playhouse
Fox, Mem. (1986). *Hattie and the Fox.*
Hogrogian, Nanny. (1971). *One Fine Day.*
Hutchins, Pat. (1968). *Rosie's Walk.*

Makeup Mess
Axelrod, Amy. (1994). *Pigs Will Be Pigs.*
Hoban, Russell. (1970). *A Bargain for Frances.*
Viorst, Judith. (1978). *Alexander, Who Used to Be Rich Last Sunday.*
Whitin, David J., and Wilde, Sandra. (1992). *Read Any Good Math Lately?*

Get Out of Bed!
Gray, Kes. (2002). *Really, Really.*
Harrison, Joanna. (1996). *When Mum Turned Into a Monster.*
McMillan, Bruce. (1989). *Time To . . .*
O'Neill, Alexis. (2002). *The Recess Queen.*

Alligator Baby
Hickman, Pamela. (2003). *Animals and Their Young: How Animals Produce and Care for Their Young.*
Lang, Aubrey. (2002). *Baby Seal.*
(And see the rest of the titles in Fitzhenry and Whiteside's Nature Babies series.)
Rockwell, Anne F. (2003). *American Alligators.*
Simon, Seymour. (2003). *Gorillas.*
Wexo, John B. (2000). *Seals and Sea Lions.*
(And see the rest of the titles in Wildlife Education Ltd.'s Zoobooks series.)
See also the All About Pets series by Capstone Press; the Science of Living Things series by Crabtree Publishing; the Wildlife Series by Kids Can Press; the Getting to Know . . . Nature's Children series by Grolier Limited/Scholastic Inc.

We Share Everything!
Adams, Cynthia. (1998). *World Famous Landmarks.*
Bemelmans, Ludwig. (1939). *Madeline.*
Hunter, Ryan Ann and Miller, Edward. (1998). *Into the Sky.*
Kalman, Bobbie. (1999). *Everyday Structures from A to Z.*

Ribbon Rescue

Bourgeois, Paulette. (1988). *Hurry Up, Franklin!*
Galdone, Paul. (1975). *The Gingerbread Boy.*
Rosen, Michael. (1989). *We're Going on a Bear Hunt.*

Biographical Information

Canadian Children's Book Centre. (1999). *The Storymakers: Illustrating Children's Books.*
Canadian Children's Book Centre. (2000). *The Storymakers: Writing Children's Books.*
Gertridge, Allison. (2002). *Meet Canadian Authors and Illustrators,* Second Edition.
Jones, Raymond and Stott, John. (2000). *Canadian Children's Books: A Critical Guide to Authors and Illustrators.*

Websites

http://www.robertmunsch.com
The author's official website.

www.scholastic.ca
Check Scholastic Canada's website for more information on Robert Munsch.

Videos

"The Life and Times of Robert Munsch" (2000) is an episode of CBC television's Life and Times series. It is designed for an adult audience, but offers interesting insights into and information about Munsch's life and work. To order, see the CBC website or phone (416) 205-6384.

"Meet the Author: Robert Munsch" (1985) is a short video from Mead Educational designed for a children's audience, with information about Munsch's life and work. It is available at most public libraries.

Additional Notes

We thank the students who generously shared their letters, stories and artwork, and the parents who kindly shared their children's photographs.

Cover and interior design by Andrea Casault

Cover and interior illustrations copyright © by Michael Martchenko except pages 27, 29, 31 and 32 copyright © by Alan and Lea Daniel; and pages 49, 50, 51, 54, and 55 copyright © by Eugenie Fernandes

Photo on page 5 by Barry Johnston

Every effort has been made to obtain permission for, and to credit appropriately, all photographs used in this book. Any further information will be appreciated and acknowledged in subsequent editions.

National Library of Canada Cataloguing in Publication

Von Heyking, Amy J. (Amy Jeanette), 1965-
Teaching with Robert Munsch books / Amy von Heyking, Janet McConaghy.

ISBN 0-439-97433-X

1. Munsch, Robert N., 1945- --Study and teaching (Elementary).
2. English language--Study and teaching (Elementary). 3. Language arts (Elementary). 4. Social sciences--Study and teaching (Elementary)--Canada.
5. Children's stories, Canadian (English)--Study and teaching (Elementary).
I. McConaghy, Janet II. Title.

PS8576.U575Z92 2003 C813'.54 C2003-901055-4
PZ7

6 5 4 3 2 1   Printed in Canada   03 04 05 06